EXPLORE YOUR CREATIVITY

ADULT COLORING BOOK

CREATED BY TIFFINI JOHNSON
copyright 2021

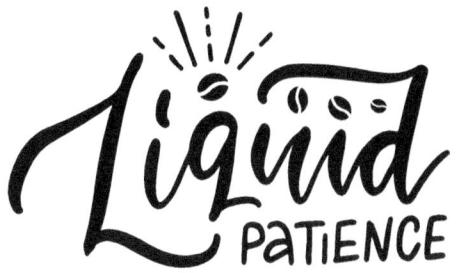

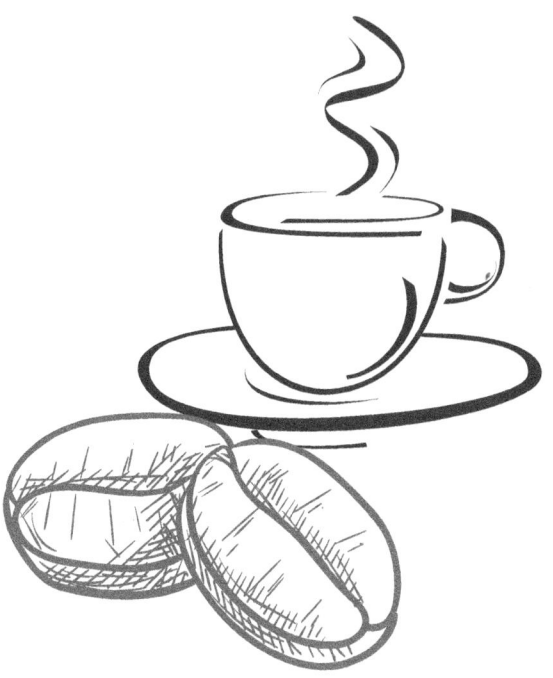

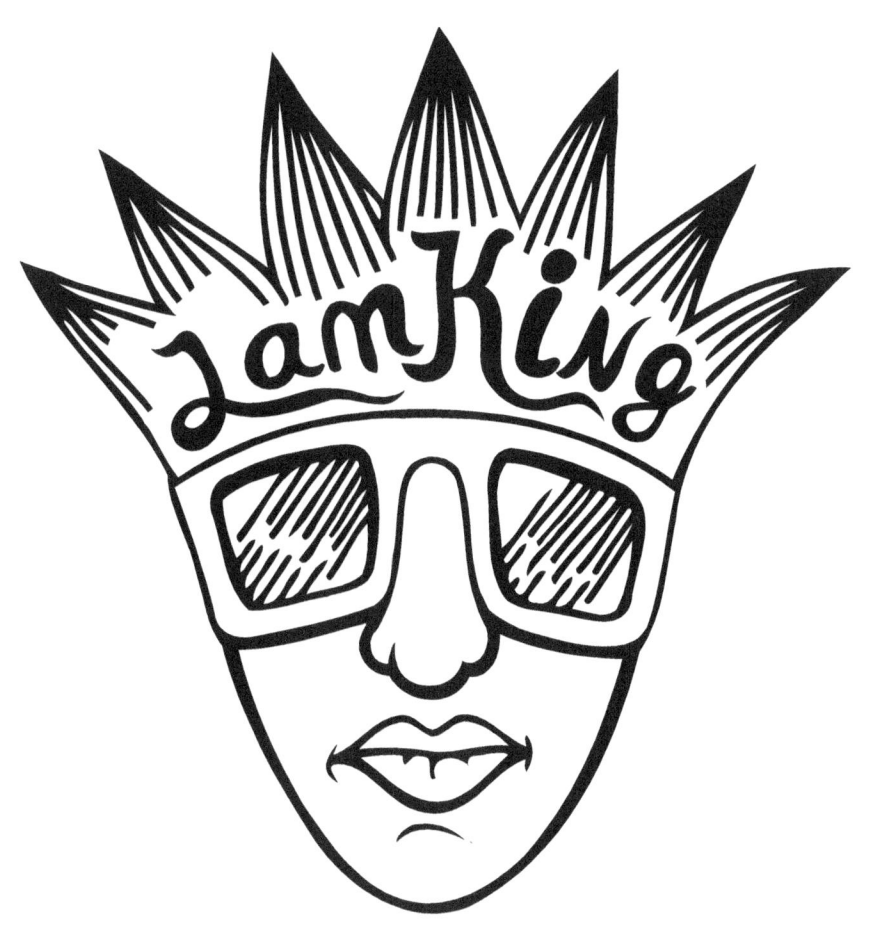

ALWAYS BELIEVE IN the impossible

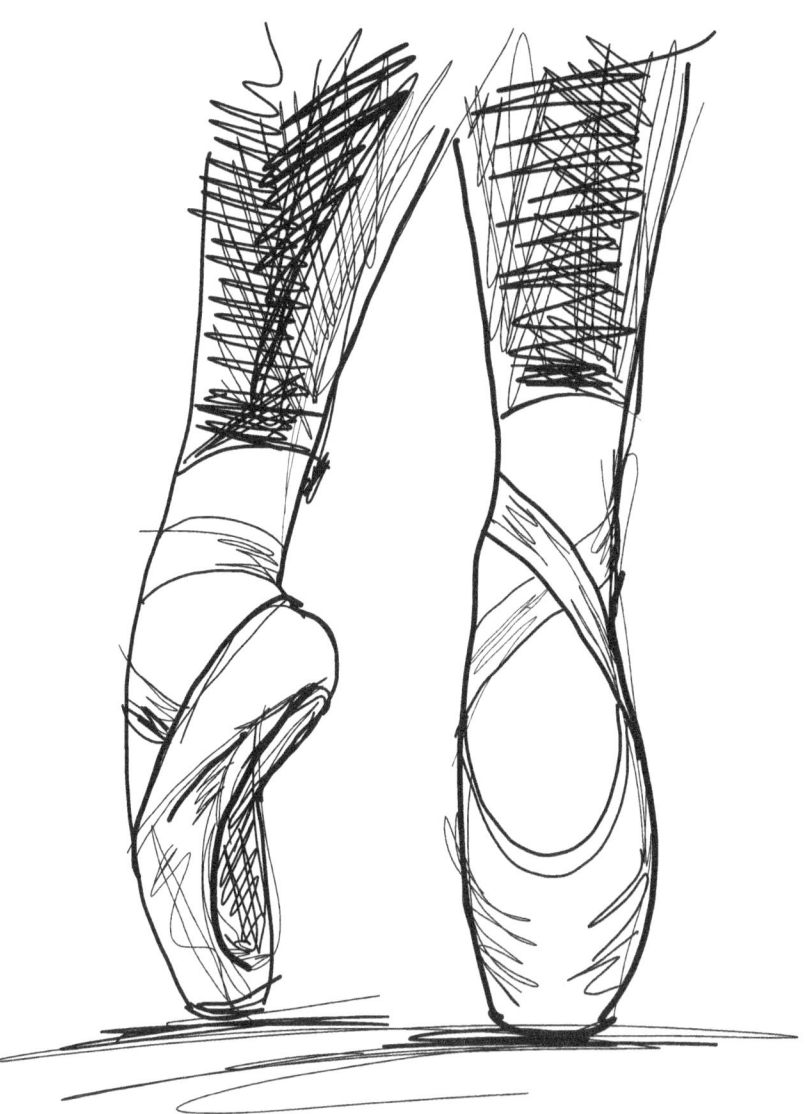

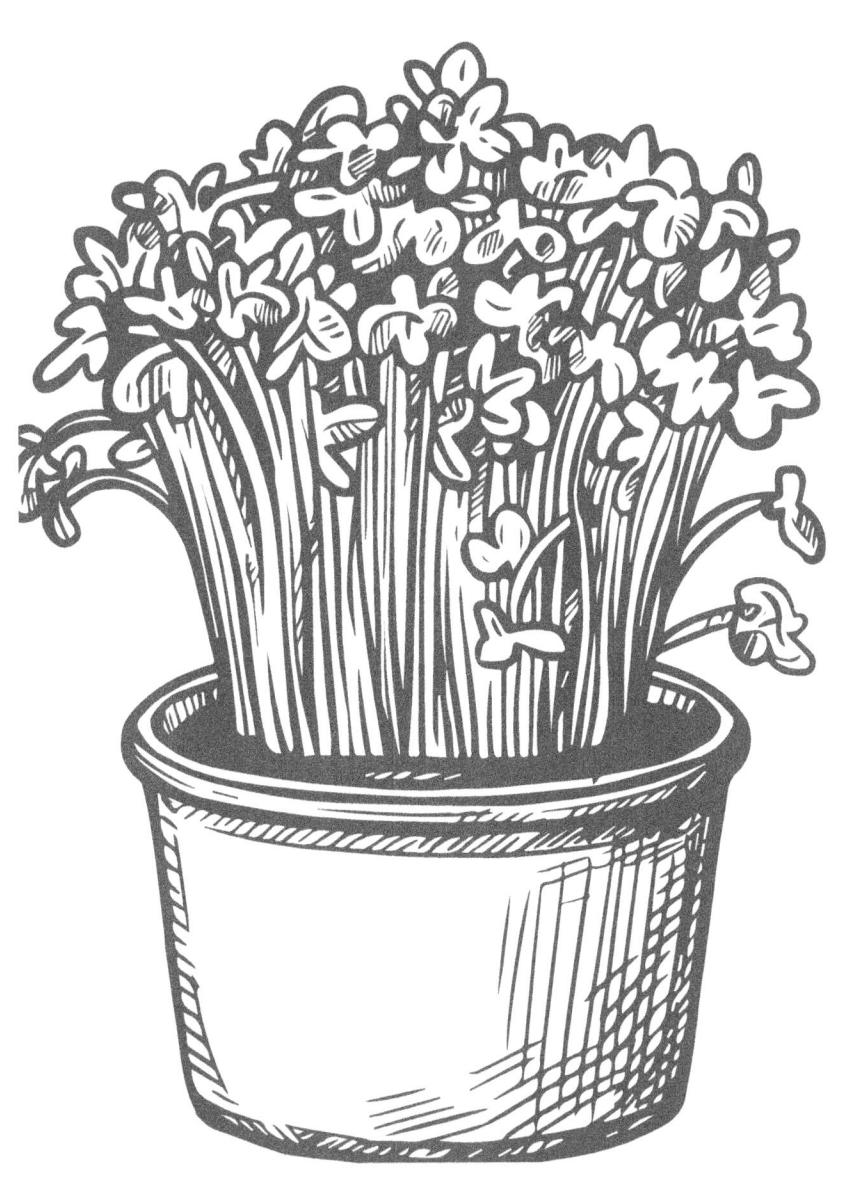

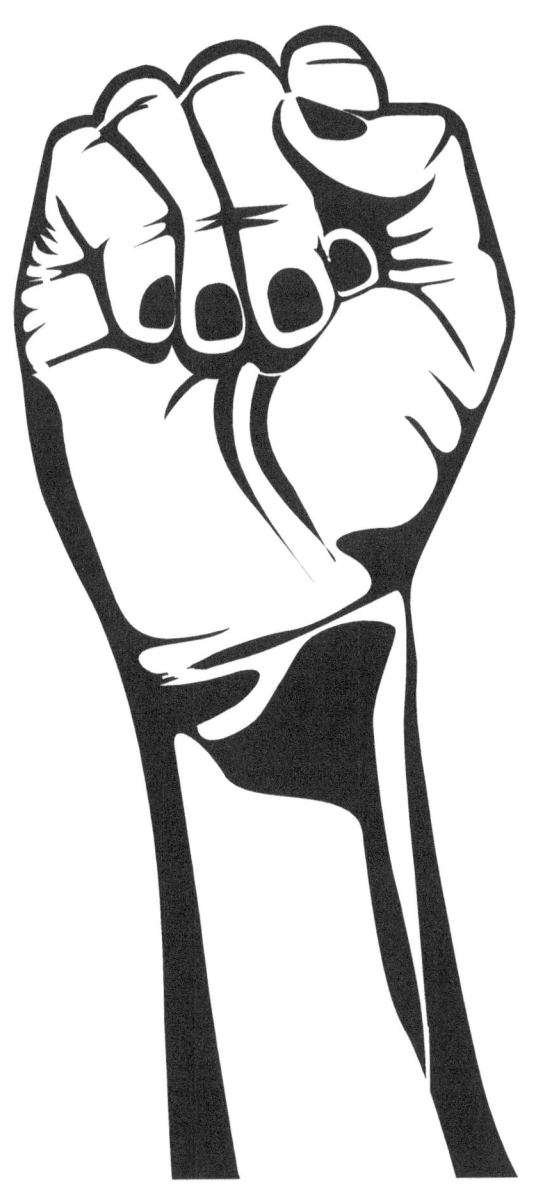

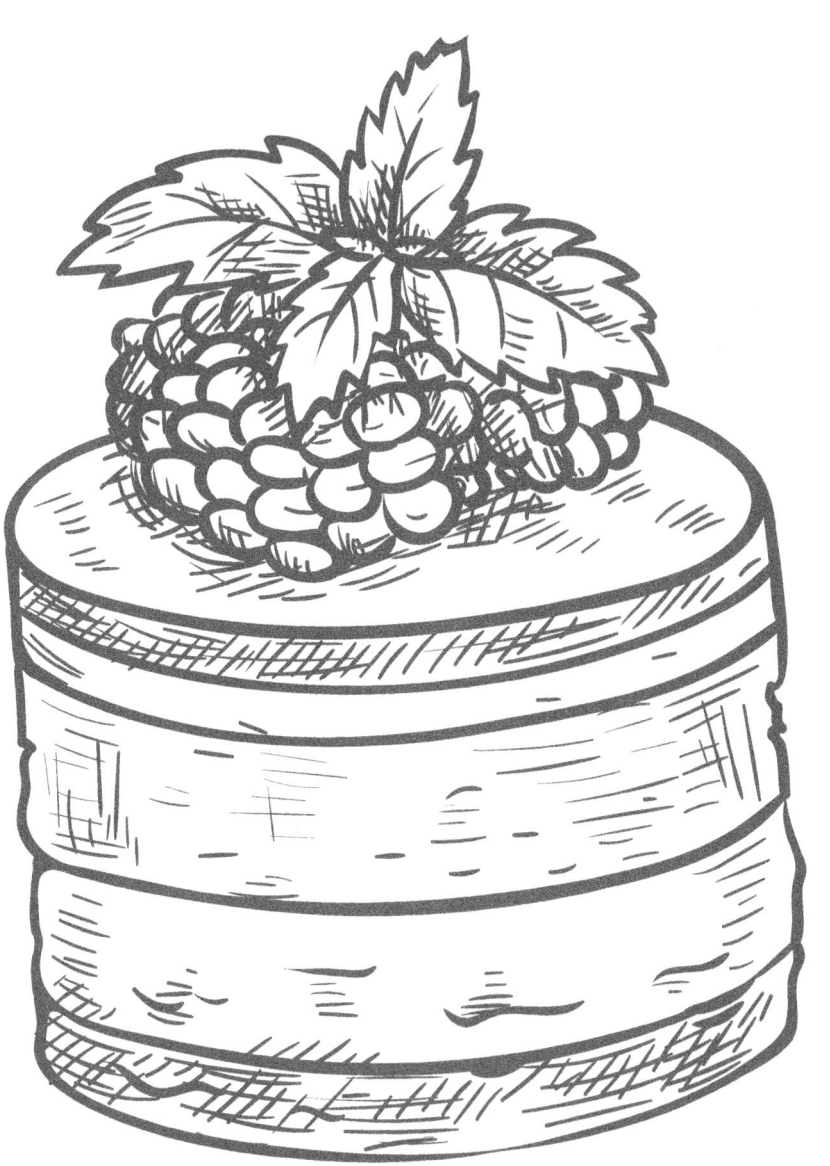

Seek Magic Everyday

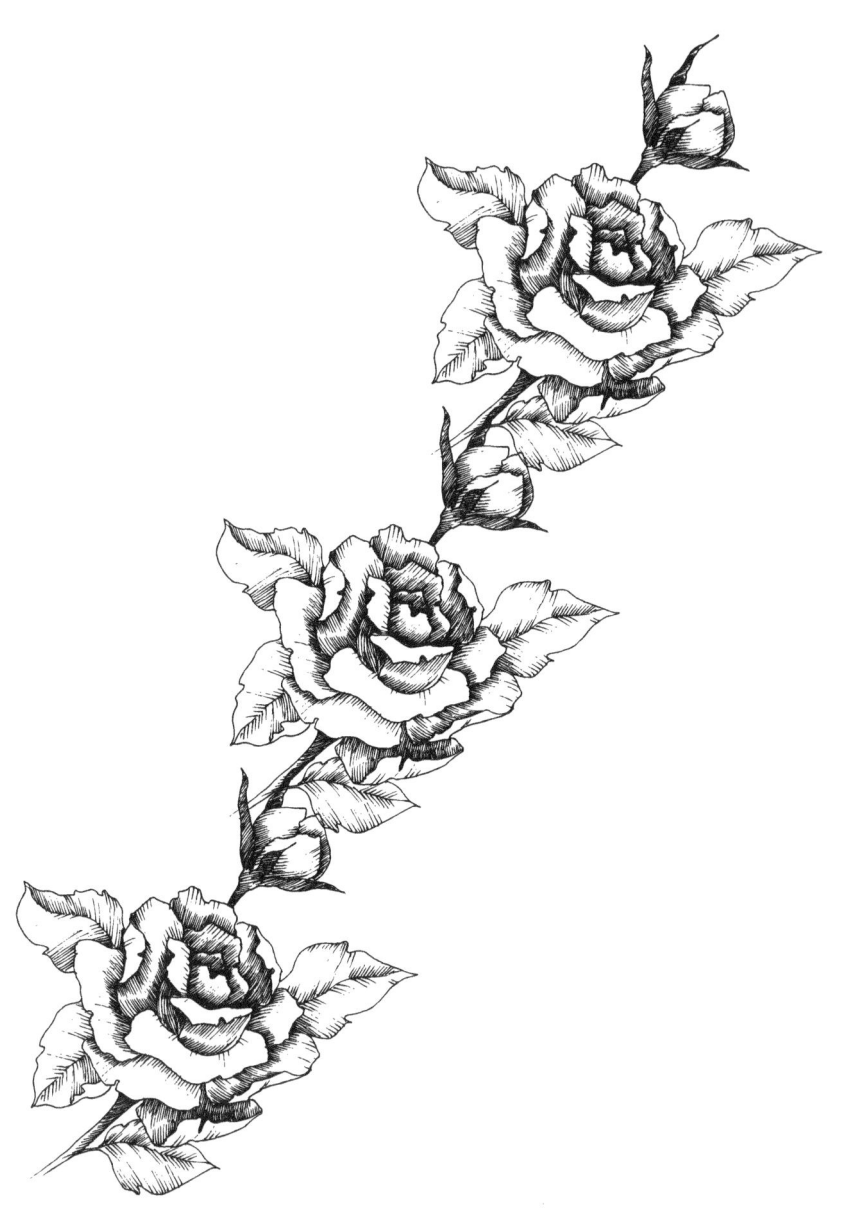

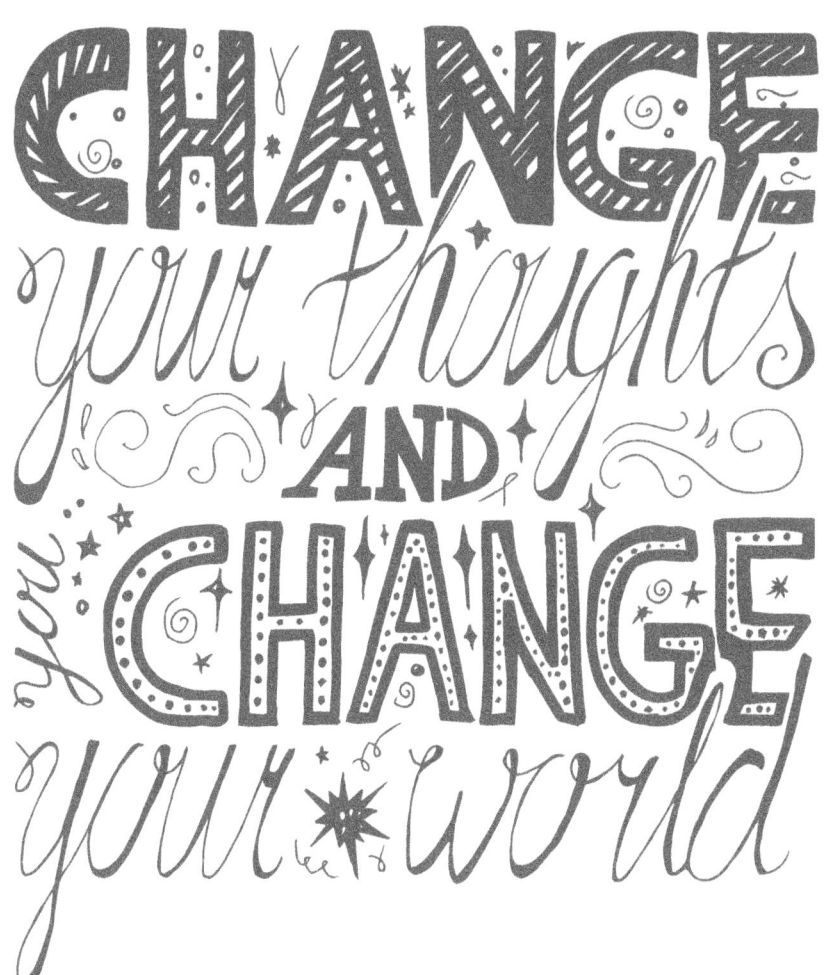

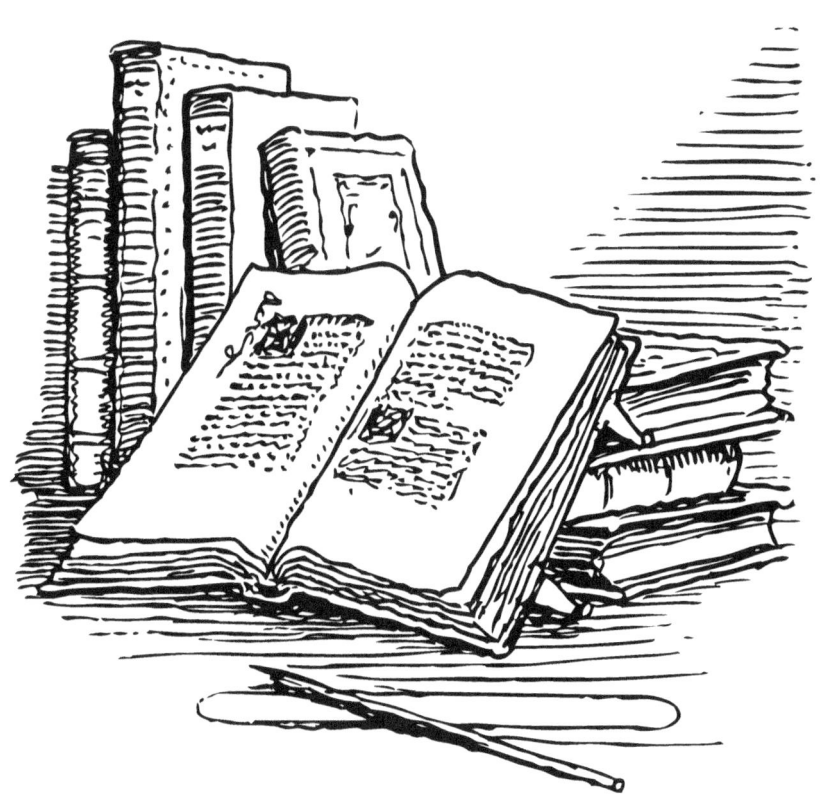

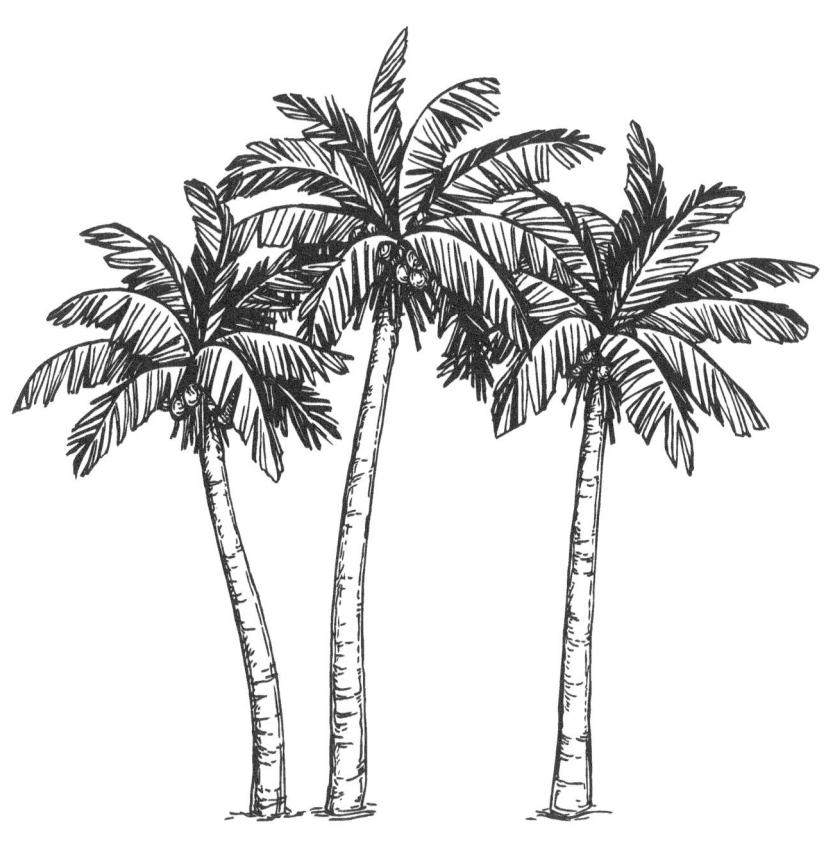

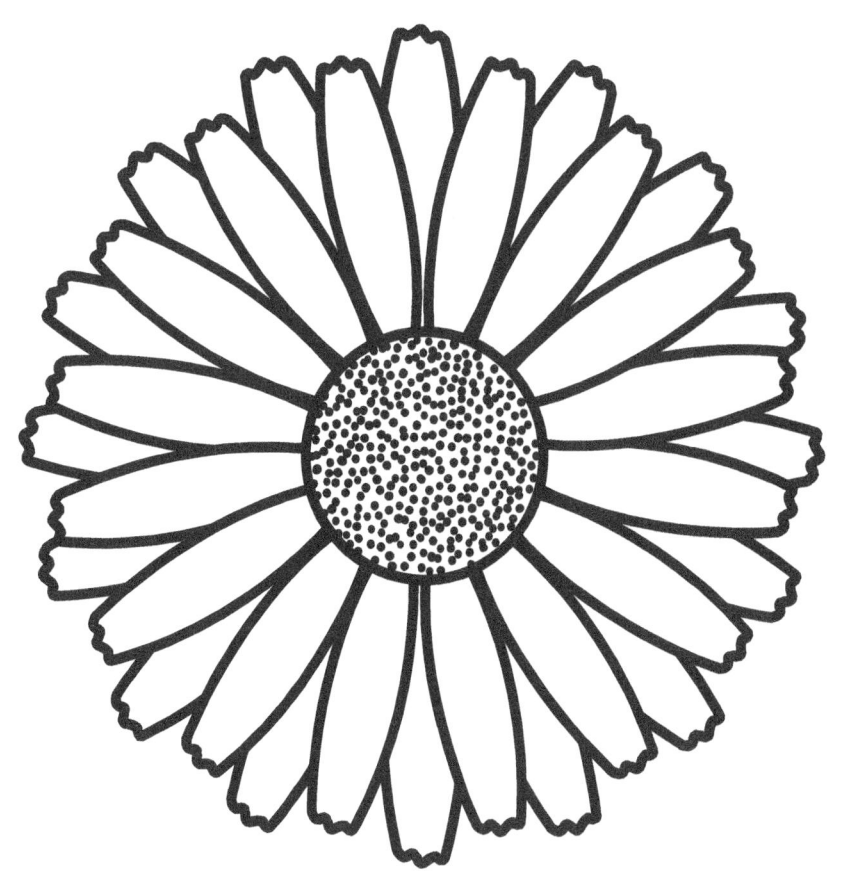

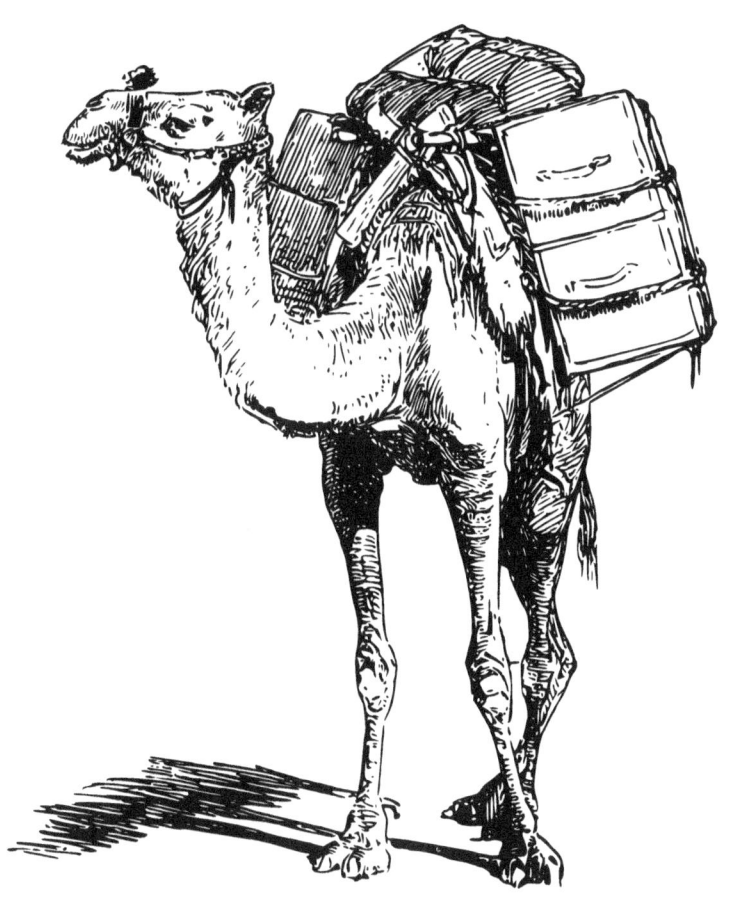

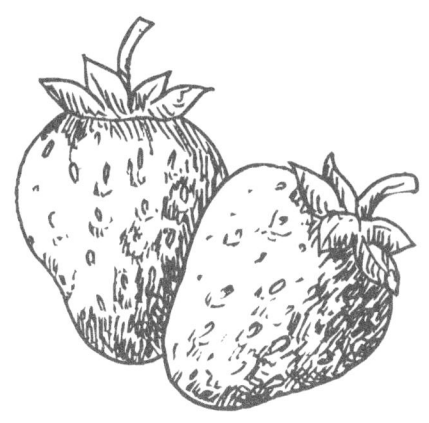

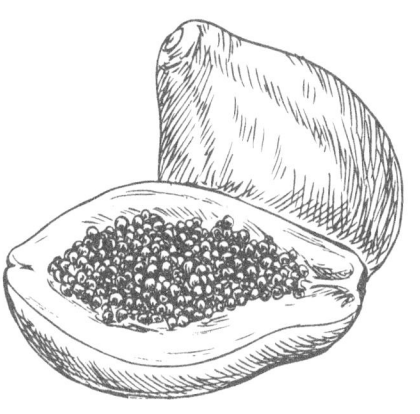

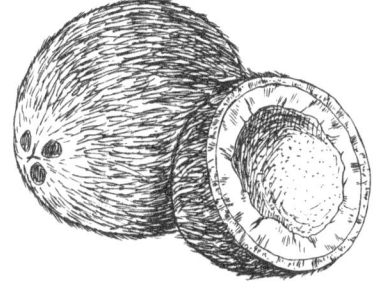

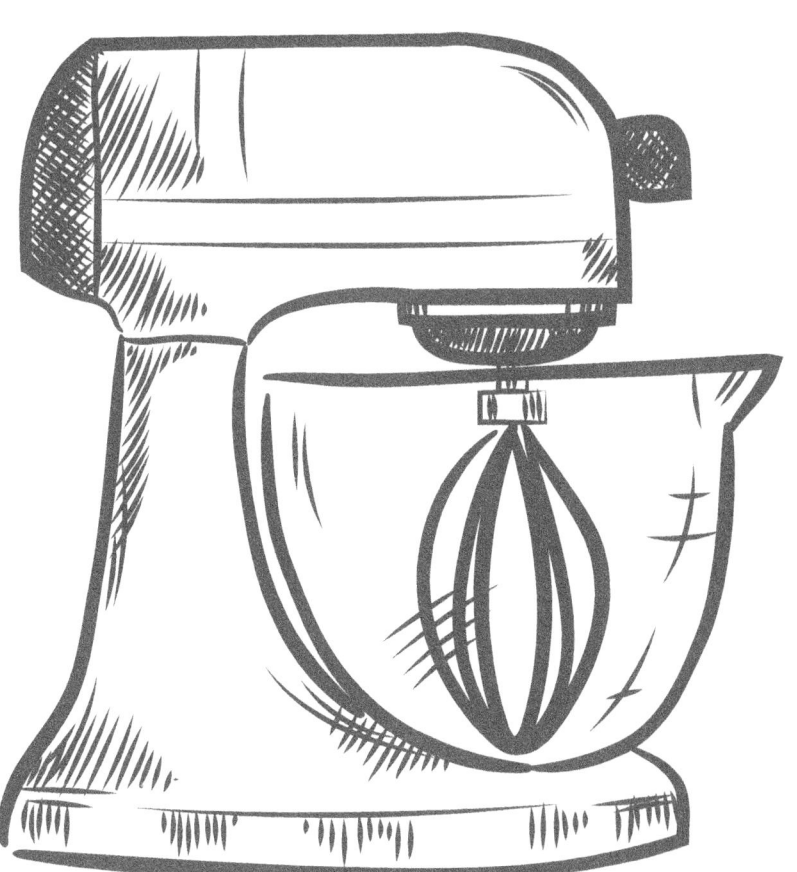

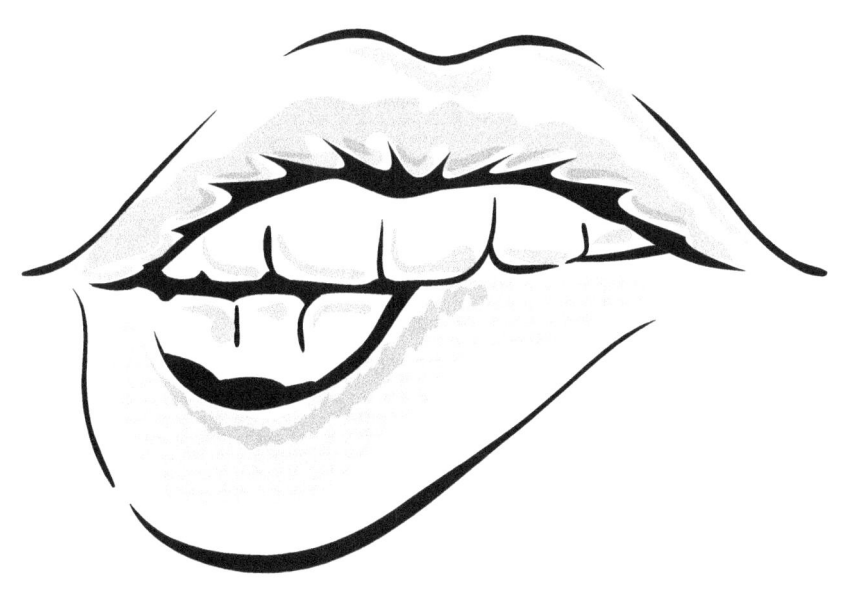

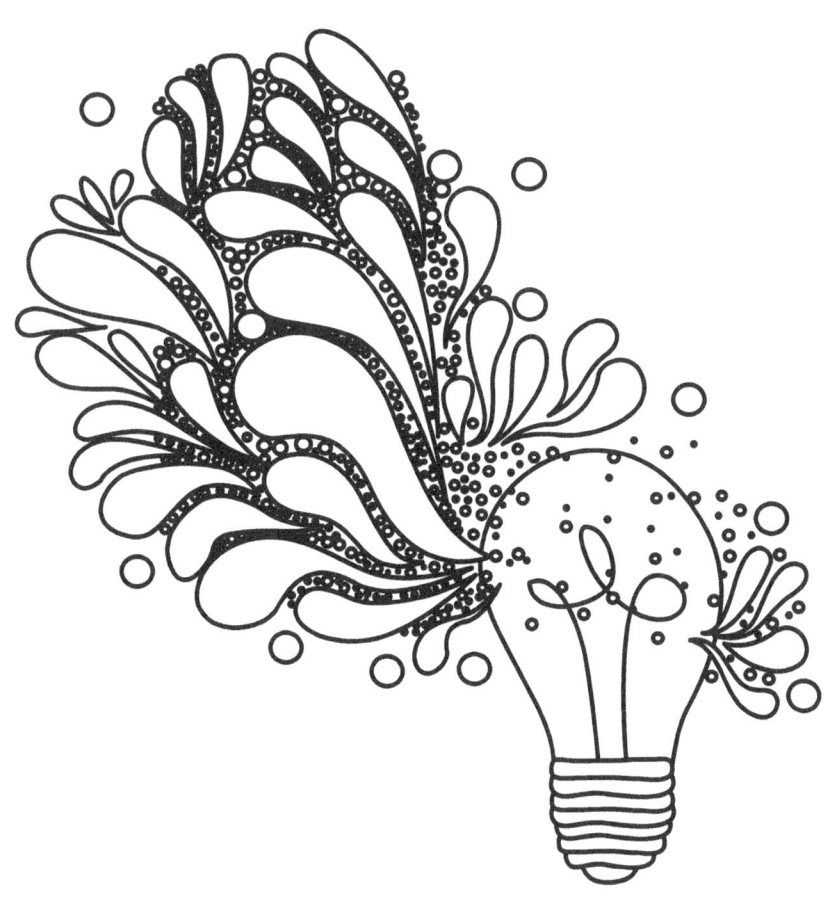

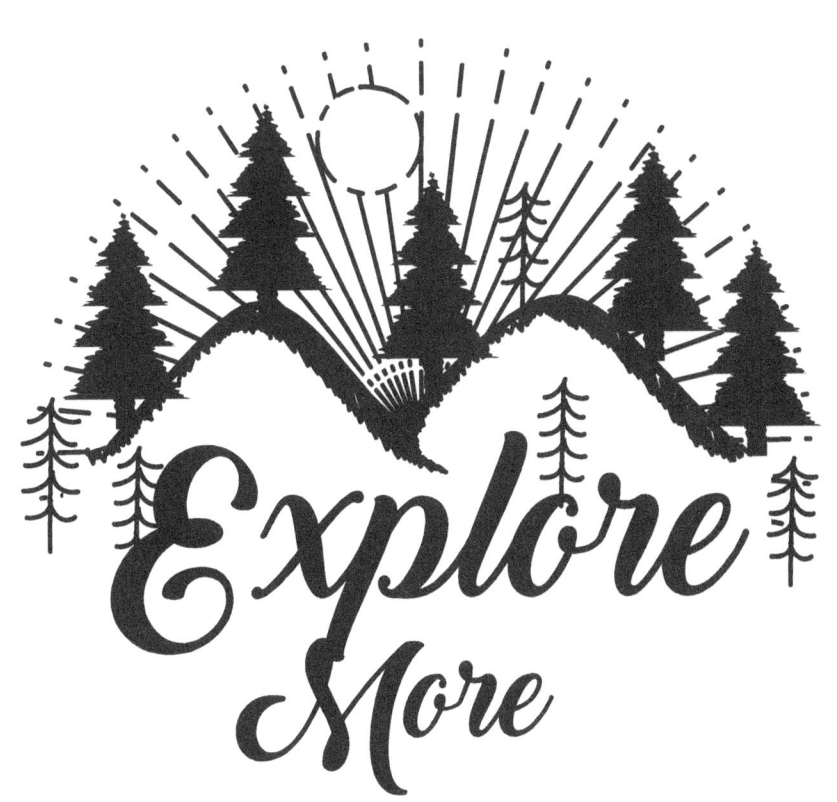

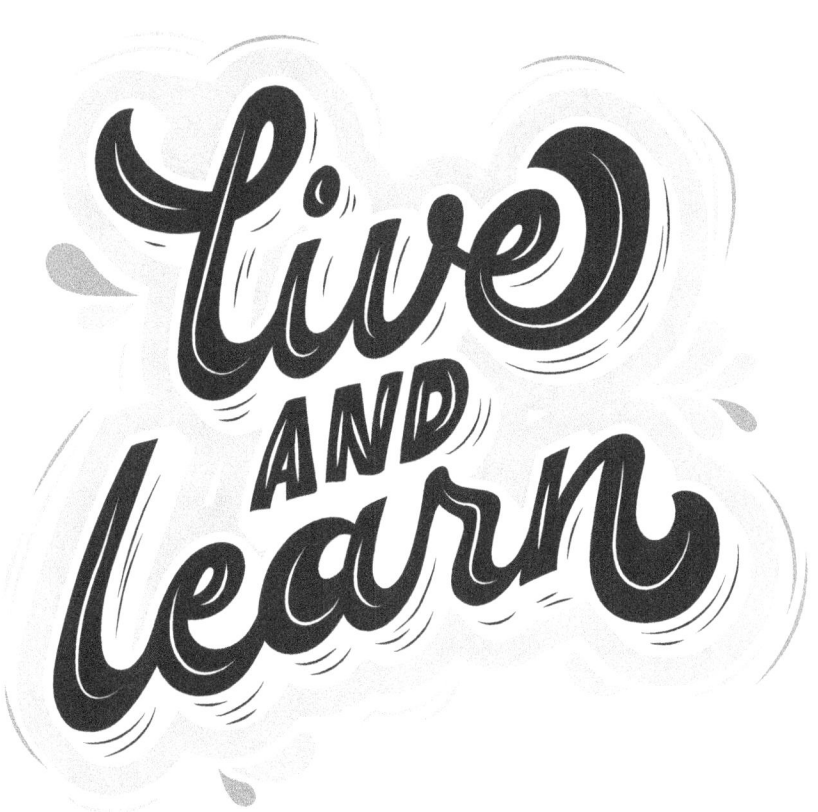

Thanks For Coloring with me!

Adult Coloring Book Created By Tiffini Johnson

www.ingramcontent.com/pod-product-compliance
Lightning Source LLC
Chambersburg PA
CBHW050320220526
45465CB00005B/2063